Ice Cream

Addition

Dona Herweck Rice

Ice cream was first made long ago.

Only rich people ate it.

Sometimes, it was made from snow and honey.

Or, it was made
from ice and fruit.

Italy had some of the first ice cream.

It was made
from cream, ice,
and fruit.

Ice cream spread around the world.

Now, we all love this cool and tasty treat!

Problem Solving

It is time for an ice cream party! Draw pictures to solve the problems.

1. There is 1 tub of ice cream. Nya brings 2 more tubs. How many tubs are there now?

2. Lee brings 3 spoons. Taj brings 4 spoons. How many total spoons are there?

3. Cal has 8 sprinkles. Some are red and some are blue. How many red and blue sprinkles could he have?

Answer Key

1. 3 tubs

2. 7 spoons

3. Answers will vary. Example: 2 red sprinkles and 6 blue sprinkles

Consultants

Nicole Belasco, M.Ed.
Kindergarten Teacher, Colonial School District

Colleen Pollitt, M.A.Ed.
Math Support Teacher, Howard County Public Schools

Publishing Credits

Rachelle Cracchiolo, M.S.Ed., *Publisher*
Conni Medina, M.A.Ed., *Managing Editor*
Dona Herweck Rice, *Series Developer*
Emily R. Smith, M.A.Ed., *Series Developer*
Diana Kenney, M.A.Ed., NBCT, *Content Director*
June Kikuchi, *Content Director*
Véronique Bos, *Creative Director*
Robin Erickson, *Art Director*
Stacy Monsman, M.A., and Karen Malaska, M.Ed., *Editors*
Michelle Jovin, M.A., *Associate Editor*
Fabiola Sepulveda, *Graphic Designer*

Image Credits: p.2 Lebrecht Music and Arts Photo Library/Alamy; p.3 Lordprice Collection/Alamy; p.8, p.13 Bridgeman Images; p.9 Look and Learn/Bridgeman Images; all other images from iStock and/or Shutterstock.

Library of Congress Cataloging-in-Publication Data

Names: Rice, Dona, author.
Title: The history of ice cream / Dona Herweck Rice.
Description: Huntington Beach, CA : Teacher Created Materials, [2019] |
   Audience: Grades K to 3.
Identifiers: LCCN 2017059897 (print) | LCCN 2017060687 (ebook) | ISBN
   9781480759589 (e-book) | ISBN 9781425856205 (pbk.)
Subjects: LCSH: Ice cream, ices, etc.--History--Juvenile literature.
Classification: LCC TX795 (ebook) | LCC TX795 .R525 2019 (print) | DDC
   641.86/2--dc23
LC record available at https://lccn.loc.gov/2017059897

Teacher Created Materials

5301 Oceanus Drive
Huntington Beach, CA 92649-1030
www.tcmpub.com

ISBN 978-1-4258-5620-5
© 2019 Teacher Created Materials, Inc.
Printed in China
Nordica.072018.CA21800711